THE RATIONAL EMOTIVE TRAIN

JOSEPH L. GILL
MS, LMFT

 FriesenPress

Suite 300 - 990 Fort St
Victoria, BC, V8V 3K2
Canada

www.friesenpress.com

ISBN
978-1-5255-7341-5 (Hardcover)
978-1-5255-7342-2 (Paperback)
978-1-5255-7343-9 (eBook)

1. BODY, MIND & SPIRIT, HEALING

Distributed to the trade by The Ingram Book Company

TABLE OF CONTENTS

WELCOME ABOARD!!

THE RATIONAL EMOTIVE TRAIN (RET) IS A DREAM train that symbolizes our power in life to make positive adjustments to emotional situations. It is powered by Happiness, Love, Trust, and Faith in the Great Creator.

The Great Creator, though known by many names and descriptions, is used here and throughout the book to describe the power that is above all things and higher than us: The Unmoved-Mover, and master decision maker of all things. All decisions made by the Great Creator have a purpose and we do not have to understand or know the reasons for them. We need to build, trust and rely on our confidence in ourselves to be able to make successful and adequate adjustments to life events. Successful living is entailed in our ability to make successful adjustments in life.

There will be no leeches, poor-me victims, prosecutor or judges allowed aboard this train. This train is headed for a new beginning of a childhood mind full of innocence and happiness. On this train we

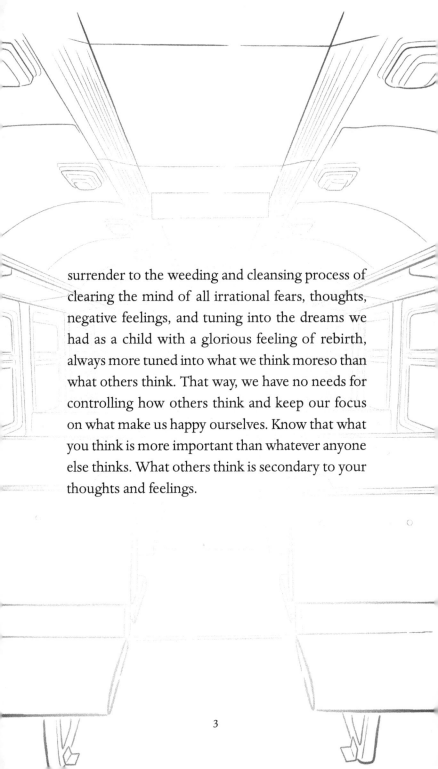

surrender to the weeding and cleansing process of clearing the mind of all irrational fears, thoughts, negative feelings, and tuning into the dreams we had as a child with a glorious feeling of rebirth, always more tuned into what we think moreso than what others think. That way, we have no needs for controlling how others think and keep our focus on what make us happy ourselves. Know that what you think is more important than whatever anyone else thinks. What others think is secondary to your thoughts and feelings.

RET COMMITMENTS

WHEN YOU RIDE THIS TRAIN THERE ARE CERTAIN commitments you can make that will make your experience and insightful gains more successful:

- Be honorable with your words and always be mindful of how you use them. If you don't have something nice to say about yourself or someone else don't say anything at all. The primary motivation in life should be to be happy and make others happy.
- Follow and have faith in your survival instincts and actions and don't look back or take others' responses personally. You cannot control how others respond or process your actions. Have confidence in your decisions; they are well assessed based on your own

personal experience that others won't always understand or might have reasons not to.

- Have faith, trust and confidence in all that you do. Focus more on what makes you happy rather than how to resolve the issues of others. Give others permission to work their issues out for themselves.

- Love yourself. Know and practice the difference between giving and sacrificing. When you give you should give willingly and have no expectations. Gratitude is nice but should not be a condition for giving other than to make others happy; that is a gracious reward. Sacrificing, on the other hand, takes away from yourself and if not under control you could easily sacrifice yourself away. And, when your self is gone, you won't be able to give to yourself or anyone else. This will defeat the act of giving.

- Don't assume anything and if by chance you do, do so with a grain of salt and pause before you act or get more clarity. Remember you are not a saint and must learn to forgive yourself when not perfect.

- Always do no more and no less than the best you can. If you try to do more than the best you can you are most likely over-compensating. If you do less, you are selling yourself short.

HAPPINESS, LOVE, FAITH, TRUST, AND CONFIDENCE.

HAPPINESS AND LOVE ARE CRUCIAL TO DEVEL- oping and sustaining rational emotions.

The key to love and happiness in life is to choose a path of balance between all opposing forces and keep the positive on the dominant side. One force cannot exist without an opposing force. Just as we regulate our exposure to opposing forces of hot and cold to a temperature that makes us comfortable, so must we moderate all forces in nature that we can control. Those we cannot are left to the regulations of the Great Creator and we must learn to make adjustments.

According to the Yin (female) / Yang (Male) principles of Tao Te Ching,

males and females are opposing forces. The male is seen as the live force and female the ground force.

It's the attraction between these forces that is essential to birth and survival of the human species and all species alike. When they connect, this is a love relationship that brings pleasure, happiness, and reproduction, which preserves the life of all living species of nature. Life is a product of love.

The key to love and happiness in life is self-regulation and moderation, which will naturally bring about a harmonious balance in all relationships.

The four essential ingredients of love are:

- trust
- vulnerability
- humility

The ability to transmit the spiritual nature of love feelings in such a way that they are felt by the ones you love.

These four ingredients can be used interchangeably and you cannot really have one without the other to and express love.

DEFENSE-SYSTEM

AS YOU VENTURE FURTHER ALONG INSIDE THE train, you will discover the Defense System Car. This car has information related to your survival mechanisms. Anxiety and Anger are opposing forces of your fight / flight, sympathetic and Para-sympathetic nervous system, both of which operate best from reflex, not from irrational fear, anticipated or self-created threats, which are unnecessary and unwarranted. Irrational and self created threats throw off the balance between your opposing forces of your natural survival mechanisms, generates a feeling of threat, and brings unnecessary dominance to your anxiety.

This is an anxiety trick that cripple and handicaps your ability to take most appropriate actions to deal with rational situations. This can:

- put a damper on your happiness
- create insomnia and interfere with a restful sleep

- Ruin your morning and create a grouchy and unhappy day unless you find a way to get a nap in.

The balance between those forces of your survival nervous system is influenced by your Superego (sense of conscience and morality) established early in life through society and your relationship with your same sex parent. By the time you become an adult if you have issues related to your Superego it should have been worked out by now or you should commit to doing so. Reconciliation of any unresolved issues you may have with your Superego will bring feelings of forgiveness and internal sense of peace. This helps to regulate a state of imbalance and minimize your Superego's influence on your anxiety and anger reactions.

A good balance between the opposing forces of your survival mechanism has an influence on your path and goals of being happy and sharing this happiness wherever you go and with whomever you make contact. Happiness is a love connection and celebration of the beauty of life and minimizes and relaxes our need for a state of defensiveness.

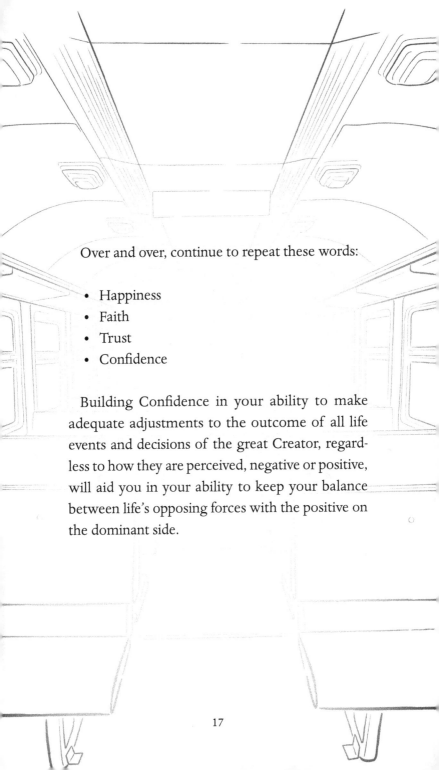

Over and over, continue to repeat these words:

- Happiness
- Faith
- Trust
- Confidence

Building Confidence in your ability to make adequate adjustments to the outcome of all life events and decisions of the great Creator, regardless to how they are perceived, negative or positive, will aid you in your ability to keep your balance between life's opposing forces with the positive on the dominant side.

EMOTIONAL MANAGEMENT

ON THIS TRAIN THERE WILL BE NO TOLERANCE for the irrational emotions of anger or anxiety. Learning to manage these emotions is mandatory.

Anger and anxiety rest on opposite ends of the same emotional pole. They both are survival mechanisms. Anger is readiness for fight and anxiety induces fear that provokes readiness for flight. These reactions become problems for individuals when they reach extreme ends of the pole. This takes the emotions to an exaggerated level.

Exaggerated anger is rage, while exaggerated fears are anxiety disorders of different descriptions. To be angry and afraid doesn't necessarily entail irrational behavior. We are capable of rational thought and limit setting under conditions of anger and fear, but not when they are at exaggerated levels of rage and irrational fear.

A distinction should be made here between anger and rage. Anger is a healthy emotion and we need it for setting limits and taking care of ourselves in stressful and frustrating situations. Anger demonstrates our boundaries and people generally respect that provided that they are reasonable. Rage is a different animal. When a person is in a state of rage, their rational brain has been hijacked and consumed by the emotion at hand. There is minimal or no access to rational thought and reason.

Similar distinctions can be made between anger and conditions of fear. Fear, like anger, is a necessary emotion. We certainly need fear to prompt us to avoid or escape situations that could do us harm. Rational fears are essential in situations of threat, especially when situations are much more powerful than we can challenge. Good sense can often tell us the distinction. Panic attacks on the other hand are irrational fears. When in a panic state, the person is actually consumed by his fear to the extent that he does not have access to rational thought, and therefore become a victim of his fear.

People with anger problems tend to be less tolerable in society than those with anxiety issues because they tend to be volatile and pose an observable physical threat. Rage is disturbing to the people around them, whereas exaggerated fears are more disturbing to the individual experiencing

them. People with anxiety problems simply make themselves less visible.

Rage and severe anxiety reactions (panic) are conditioned responses to a perceived threat that resembles past experiences that drew strong emotions in a situation where the person felt powerless, overwhelmed, and had no escape.

The rage reactions provide an adrenaline rush that gives an immediate elevated sense of power in a situation whereby the person feels that they have no power. They are taken to a power zone they never knew existed. They appear crazy to the observer, but to themselves, they feel elevated and above the problem. When the adrenaline settles down, there are some feelings of guilt at first, but it is relieved. Each time the reaction is triggered, it becomes easier to be ignited the next time. As the reaction repeats itself the tolerance for frustration in general is lowered.

Rage is a sign of absence in humility and lack of trust in the Great Creator. Persons who lack trust or humility and only trust themselves generally focus on their ability to control all outcomes in life.

On this train they are encouraged to build or restore their trust in the Great Creator and build a level of reliance on their relationship with the above. Persons who struggle with anger and rage problems would do well to include the serenity prayer in their

commitments. Simply ask the great Creator, "Grant me the serenity to accept the things I cannot change, courage to change the things I can, and wisdom to know the difference." I think it can be found to be useful in times of emotional turmoil.

Anxiety and worry are indication of diminished faith and trust in the Great Creator. It is an attempt to take control of outcomes of which you have no control. To reduce this state of mind you must learn to relax and restore your trust and faith, and build your confidence in your ability to adjust to unforeseen outcomes that are entirely in the hands of the Great Creator. You must stop trying the control the outcome of in events that you do not have control over. Learn to relax and let go. The Great Creator decides what's best for all things. Move with the flow of life forces. Balance between the opposing forces of nature is the key to love and happiness. Keep your balance between the opposing forces of life and nature.

You can be your own best friend or worst enemy. Anxiety teams up with your worst enemy...And when the anxiety monster climbs on your shoulders or invades your heart, always remember there are two sides to every coin.

On the head side is your own best friend. On the tail side is your own worst enemy. Make the decision to dismiss the tail side of the coin. It wrings

out all the past and present negative and pessimistic thoughts that keep you awake at night. Then embrace the head side where your own best friend reside and points out the positive and optimistic ways of viewing your thoughts and concerns whatever they may be, and gives support to your love for yourself.

Believe it or not most chronic worriers, unconsciously, worry most about forgetting what they are worried about so they habitually rehearse their worries over and over. To break this habit you should make yourself a worry list, fold it and keep it in your pocket. Only take it out when you want to take the time out for it. This way you become in charge of your worries rather than your worries taking charge of you or your thoughts.

CRYING AND LAUGHTER

WHEN EXPERIENCING OR ATTEMPTING TO manage emotional struggles, such as anger and anxiety, we often tend to overlook our body's own natural resources and strong emotional liberators: crying and laughter.

Increased access to both could work towards a reduction in both anxiety and anger. Crying and laughter are emotional outlets we are born with. They are inborn emotional stress releasers that tend to boost the activity of the immune system. They release endorphins and can increase antibodies that help combat strong emotions.

Laboratory studies of the composition of emotional tears have found that they contain high levels of adrenocorticotropic (ATCH), a hormone released in the body when under stress. Tears may release emotional stress by effectively shedding these hormones while crying.

Anyone that has had a good cry can testify to its healing powers and how much better they feel afterwards, especially in times of strong disappointment and emotional loss. Crying, with or without tears, tends to be a natural outlet for managing sadness, grief and disappointment. People who are afraid to cry don't know what they are missing in terms a valuable form of relief and emotional outlet. Depending on the intensity, crying involves compulsive rhythmic contractions of major muscle groups that are followed by a relaxed state.

The principles of rhythmic contractions of major muscle groups followed by a relaxed state can also be seen at work in laughter. Laughter, in reality, is the antithesis to the stress response. That is, it is impossible to laugh and be stressed at the same time. In contrast to anger, which evokes the fight-flight response, laughter dismantles it by reducing the amount of hormones such as adrenocorticotropic (ATCH) which activate the release of cortisol in the body during times of stress. In addition to pumping the heart and muscles of the chest, shoulders and neck, it also stimulates the brain, ventilates the lungs, raises the heart rate, blood pressure, respiration, and circulation.

Learning to improve one's sense of humor improves ones ability to manage stress and desensitize stress in times of strong emotional situations.

Humor (which draws laughter), if used appropriately can provide laughter while changing our focus and minimizing the intensity of our stressful emotions.

A word of caution is called for here in regards to improper use of humor. If used inappropriately, humor can become a faulty ego-defense mechanism to avoid dealing with serious situations that demand our attention. Used improperly, it can be employed to amuse or uplift our own selves at the expense of stereotyping and putting others down.

You can't cure cancer by laughing 50 times a day, but it will provide a lift in your sprits in such a way that it sure to make a contribution to your health. Here are some guidelines for bringing more humor and laughter in your life.

- Go deep when you laugh, don't be afraid to get into it.
- Learn to let go, lighten up, and look at the flip side of a situation. Laughing could keep you from crying if you had a choice.
- Play tickle games with your kid, nieces and nephews.

- Watch comedy movies with friends.
- Do something absurd to get a laugh like wearing a funny nose.
- Cut cartoons out of the funny papers and share them.
- Listen to comedy podcast while commuting, cooking or doing chores.
- Increase your daily chuckles.

THE CABOOSE CAR
AND RELAXATION

AS IS CUSTOMARY FOR A CABOOSE CAR, THE RET Caboose car rest on the back of the train where eventually it will be left behind. No longer practical for the Continental railroad, their original Caboose car now rest in a Texas museum where it belongs.

The RET Caboose car will be used to increase your ability to relax and put away haunting disturbing thoughts. Past negativity and mistakes may be difficult to clear out of your mind but they can be pushed to the back of the train where they will eventually fall off or stay locked in the darkness of the Caboose car leaving the mind free to love and dwell upon its wondrous and spiritual self.

Relaxation is a symbol of letting go. Give your body permission to let go of your mind, follow its course rather than trying to control it. Reduce anything you envision as a threat. Trust that the

opposing forces of your survival nervous system will naturally regulate themselves and activate on an as needed basis.

When the mind is cleared by the clouds of tranquility of all negative thoughts and irrational fears it is replaced with happiness, love, faith and trust, and confidence that you will be able to make satisfactory adjustments to the outcome of all events and decisions made by the Great creator and master decision maker of all things.

It's important to practice deep breathing. Deep breathing brings fresh oxygen to the brain, which sends relaxation signals to the body. This induces heaviness in the body as it relaxes, beginning with your feet, and continues up the body to the regions of your head.

When the entire body is relaxed it lets go of its grip on the mind and releases it to free associate and dwell upon its wondrous and spiritual self. This allows the mind to venture into the universe and float on the clouds of tranquility. The clouds cleanse and bring peace to the mind, relieving it of all its negative and irrational thoughts. This refreshes the mind and allows the body to fully rejuvenate and induces a rewarding nap, meditation or relaxing night's sleep.

COMMIT TO LIVE IN THE PRESENT

TO LOVE AND LIVE IN THE PRESENT IS THE BEST way to demonstrate and show gratitude to the Great Creator and not waste time and precious moments on the past. Set boundaries on your mind for the extent or time allowed to entertain or ruminate about the past or future unless you are collecting information you can actually use in the present. Ruminating on the past or future for the sake of ruminating is a counter productive is a total and often depressing waste of time.

Give the present the dominant occupation of your mind at all times. When you find or catch yourself drifting into the past or future bring up a stop sign or red light and come back to the present. The present is life and if you love your gift of life you will function and value the present.

Staying in the present is what will give you peace of mind and the love of life. Give the present dominance over the past or future especially if the thoughts are negative or dull. This is how you show the Great Creator your appreciation and gratitude for your wondrous and beautiful life. There are no stop signs or red lights in the present only green lights. Green is the sign of life growth in the present.

The present is here. The past is gone and negativity happily gone, while the future may or may not come. Invest your energy and precious thoughts in the present to grow and sustain a happy, loving and graceful life.

GRATITUDE

MORE IMPORTANT THAN ASKING THE ONE ABOVE for what we want is giving gratitude for what we receive. Not only are we given life but all the essentials for sustaining life, including the air we breathe, the sun that brings us energy, and the clouds that brings the rain.

Be thankful for a beautiful body that is full of wonderful and self-sustaining essential organs that keep us alive. We have a glorious and creative mind that is more powerful than the most sophisticated computers. We have wonderful organs and limbs that allow us to function gracefully upon earth above all other living beings. The list of all we have to be thankful for is unlimited and a true compilation of LOVE from the Great Creator.

SERENITY

IN THE SERENITY CAR, ON THIS TRAIN, WE LEARN the power and benefits of serenity. Serenity begins with a humble posture and giving thanks to a power that is higher than us. It is a feeling of peace and balance between the opposing forces of nature that gives us life. When in a state of serenity we feel a safe and secure connection with nature and ourselves. Just to be able to tune into nature's beautiful gifts through our primary senses is enough to keep us happy and appreciate life. Not only can we appreciate the life we have and live, but also the spirits of life that those whom we have loved so much, have left behind.

So, as we come to the close of our Rational Emotive Train ride, take this time to embrace the moment. Place both feet flat on the floor with your back and spine straight. Relax, close your eyes, open your heart, and breathe deeply. Enjoy that warm and comfortable feeling of serenity and tranquility. It's a rewarding and sensational feeling of love, peace, and happiness.

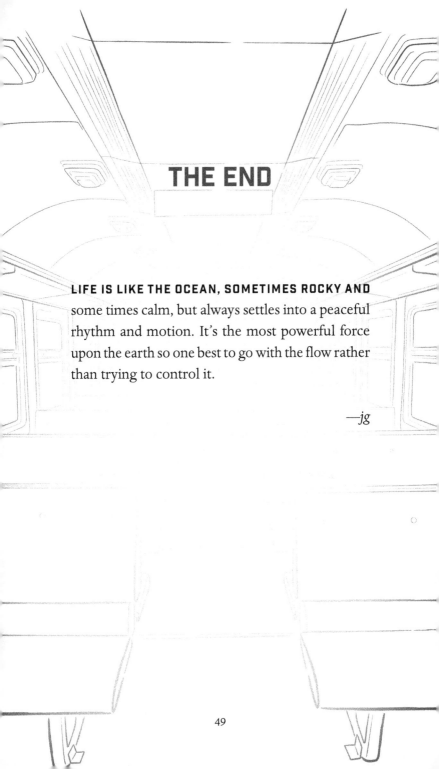

THE END

LIFE IS LIKE THE OCEAN, SOMETIMES ROCKY AND some times calm, but always settles into a peaceful rhythm and motion. It's the most powerful force upon the earth so one best to go with the flow rather than trying to control it.

—*jg*

REFERENCES OR SUGGESTED READINGS

Gill, J. L. (2004). Personalized Stress Management. Otsego, MI: PageFree Publishing.

Gill, J. L. (2018). The spirit of Oneness. San Bernardino, CA: Amazon Kindle.

The Relaxation Experience. [CD-ROM] CCSPublications, P.O.B0X 9611 SJ,CA CA 95157.

Miguel Angel Ruiz (1997). The Four Agreements. San Rafael, CA: Amber-Allen Publishing.

Richard Carlson (1997). Don't Sweat the Small Stuff. NewYork, NY: MJF Books.

Simon & Schuster (2028). Happiness Hacks. Avon, Ma: Adams Media.

ABOUT THE AUTHOR

JOSEPH L. GILL is a licensed marriage and family therapist and a former lecturer/adjunct professor at San Jose State University. He has taught courses in stress diversity and health, and he is a prominent clinician with over thirty years' experience. He also provides stress-management services on an individual and corporate level for many employee assistance programs in the San Francisco and South Bay Area. He is the author of Personalized Stress Management, The Spirit of Oneness, and The Relaxation Experience. He lives in San Jose, California.

CPSIA information can be obtained
at www.ICGtesting.com
Printed in the USA
LVHW070743101220
672134LV00042B/1041/J

9 781525 573415